Telephone to Smartphones

Then to Now Tech

By Jennifer Colby

21st Century Junior Library

Published in the United States of America by
Cherry Lake Publishing
Ann Arbor, Michigan
www.cherrylakepublishing.com

Content Adviser: Adam Fulton Johnson, PhD History of Science and Technology, University of Michigan
Reading Adviser: Marla Conn, MS, Ed., Literacy specialist, Read-Ability, Inc.

Photo Credits: ©Everett Collection/Shutterstock.com, Cover, 1 [left]; ©bysora/Shutterstock.com, Cover, 2 [right]; ©Andrii Kobryn/Shutterstock.com, 4; Library of Congress, LC-DIG- hec-15693, 6; ©Everett Historical/Shutterstock.com, 8; ©Everett Collection/Shutterstock.com, 10; Library of Congress, LC-DIG-fsa-8d32048 , 12; ©Everett Collection/Shutterstock.com, 14; ©blackzheep/Shutterstock.com, 16; ©Santi S/ Shutterstock.com, 18; ©dolphfyn/Shutterstock.com, 20

Library of Congress Cataloging-in-Publication Data
Names: Colby, Jennifer, 1971- author.
Title: Telephone to smartphones / Jennifer Colby.
Description: Ann Arbor : Cherry Lake Publishing, [2019] | Series: Then to now tech | Includes bibliographical references and index.
Identifiers: LCCN 2019004229| ISBN 9781534147256 (hardcover) | ISBN 9781534148680 (pdf) | ISBN 9781534150119 (pbk.) | ISBN 9781534151543 (hosted ebook)
Subjects: LCSH: Telephone systems–History–Juvenile literature.
Classification: LCC TK6165 .C65 2019 | DDC 621.38609–dc23
LC record available at https://lccn.loc.gov/2019004229

Cherry Lake Publishing would like to acknowledge the work of the Partnership for 21st Century Skills.
Please visit *www.p21.org* for more information.

Printed in the United States of America

CONTENTS

Today it is easy to connect with someone.

Can We Talk?

Throughout history, people have tried to communicate with others in many different ways. Can you imagine a time when you could not pick up a phone and talk with someone? People had to communicate through letters. It could take weeks to get an answer from someone!

There are many inventors to thank for the invention of the telephone.

Who was the first to invent the telephone?

First to File

Antonio Meucci, an Italian **immigrant**, made drawings of a telephone-like device in 1871. He intended to get a **patent**, but could not afford to. He lost his claim to the invention.

Five years later, both Elisha Gray of Ohio and Alexander Graham Bell, a Scottish immigrant, filed their drawings of telephone inventions at the patent office. They did it

This device was used as an early model for Bell's telephone. It transferred sound for the first time in June of 1875.

on the same day, February 14, 1876, but Bell's plan was filed first! So he gets all the credit for inventing the telephone.

As a person speaks into a telephone, an electric current carries sound waves to the listener's telephone. There were two main parts to Bell's telephone, a **transmitter** and a **receiver**.

Look!

Do you have a **landline** telephone in your house? It is connected to other phones through a series of wires. Not many people have them anymore. Ask an adult to help you look on the internet to find photos of old telephones.

Operators were needed to connect calls.

Getting in Touch

Now that the telephone was invented, people needed a way to connect their calls. The first telephone line and the first **switchboard** were constructed in the late 1870s. Soon almost 49,000 telephones were in use in the United States. Everybody wanted to talk over the phone!

Lots of telephone wires became common on city streets.

At first, there were many **independent** phone systems. You couldn't just pick up the phone and talk to anyone. Not all telephone line **networks** were connected. But soon, miles and miles of telephone wire connected phones all around the country.

Make a Guess!

Today, most people use cell phones. But when were they first invented? Make a guess. Ask others what they think.

Say hello! While speaking with someone across the world may seem like no big deal today, back in the early 1900s it seemed nearly impossible.

By 1956, the first transatlantic telephone **cable** was laid on the Atlantic Ocean floor from Scotland to Canada. For the first time, people could make a telephone call to someone across the ocean! In its first day of service, the new underwater line transmitted about 700 international calls.

Soon there were over 160 million phones connected worldwide. By 1980, there were over 175 million telephone **subscribers** in the United States alone!

Cell phone towers transmit radio waves.

On the Go

In 1991, the first 2G digital cell phone network was available in Europe. In 1993, text messaging services were introduced. Only two years later, there were 33 million cell phone subscribers in the United States. 3G technology launched in 2001 due to a growing need to access the internet. This was followed shortly after by the faster 4G and 5G networks of today.

Cell phone technology has gone through many changes.

Today over two-thirds of the world's population connect with mobile devices. Most people now use smartphones. A smartphone is a lot more powerful than early cell phones. Besides communicating with friends and family, you can use it to do all sorts of tasks. It is a mini-computer!

Ask Questions!

People in your family grew up without a cell phone. Ask them how they communicated without them. Ask if they think it is better to have, or not have, a cell phone.

A transparent smartphone may be in your future.

Smartphone technology is always evolving. Someday they could be **flexible** or even foldable to be more **portable**. One thing is for sure, smartphones will become more popular as more people around the world connect with each other.

Think!

What new features would you like in a smartphone? Share your ideas with others.

GLOSSARY

cable (KAY-buhl) a group of wires used to carry electrical signals

flexible (FLEK-suh-buhl) capable of bending

immigrant (IM-ih-gruhnt) someone who moves from one country to another and settles there

independent (in-dih-PEN-duhnt) separate from and not connected to other things

landline (LAND-line) a telephone connected by cables laid across land, either on poles or buried underground

networks (NET-wurks) systems of connected lines and wires

patent (PAT-uhnt) a legal document that gives the inventor of an item the sole rights to make and sell it

portable (POR-tuh-buhl) easy to carry or move around

receiver (rih-SEE-vur) the part of a telephone that you pick up and hold near your ear to hear what is being sent from a transmitter

subscribers (suhb-SKRIBE-urz) people who pay money regularly for a product or service

switchboard (SWICH-bord) a system used to connect telephone calls from many separate phone lines

transmitter (trans-MIT-ur) the part of a telephone that converts sound waves into electric waves that can be sent to a receiver

FIND OUT MORE

BOOKS

Carson, Mary Kay. *Alexander Graham Bell for Kids: His Life and Inventions with 21 Activities*. Chicago, IL: Chicago Review Press, 2018.

Klepeis, Alicia. *How Smartphones Work*. New York, NY: Cavendish Square, 2018.

WEBSITES

DK Find Out!—Alexander Graham Bell

https://www.dkfindout.com/us/science/famous-scientists/alexander-graham-bell
Find out more about the inventor of the telephone.

Wonderopolis—How Does a Phone Work?

https://wonderopolis.org/wonder/how-does-a-phone-work
Learn more about the evolution of phones.

INDEX

ABOUT THE AUTHOR

Jennifer Colby is a school librarian in Ann Arbor, Michigan. She loves reading, traveling, and going to museums to learn about new things.